GENE BARRETTA

LINCOLN

☆ ☆ ☆ ☆ ☆ ☆ ☆ AND ☆ ☆ ☆ ☆ ☆ ☆ ☆

KENNEDY

A PAIR TO COMPARE

Christy Ottaviano Books

HENRY HOLT AND COMPANY
NEW YORK

A special thank-you to Thomas Fleming, Benjamin Goldberg, Bill Barretta,
Claire Easton, Bill Ochester, and John Desiderio.

Henry Holt and Company, LLC
Publishers since 1866
175 Fifth Avenue, New York, New York 10010
mackids.com

Library of Congress Cataloging-in-Publication Data
Names: Barretta, Gene, author.
Title: Lincoln and Kennedy : a pair to compare / Gene Barretta.
Description: New York : Henry Holt and Company, 2016.
Identifiers: LCCN 2015026166 | ISBN 9780805099454 (hardcover)
Subjects: LCSH: Lincoln, Abraham, 1809–1865—Juvenile literature. | Kennedy, John F. (John Fitzgerald),
1917–1963—Juvenile literature. | Presidents—United States—Biography—Juvenile literature.
Classification: LCC E457.2 .B235 2016 | DDC 973.09/9—dc23
LC record available at http://lccn.loc.gov/2015026166

Our books may be purchased in bulk for promotional, educational, or business use.
Please contact your local bookseller or the Macmillan Corporate and Premium Sales Department at (800) 221-7945 ext. 5442
or by e-mail at MacmillanSpecialMarkets@macmillan.com.

First Edition—2016 / Designed by April Ward & Anna Booth
Watercolor on Arches cold-press paper was used to create the illustrations for this book.
Printed in China by RR Donnelley Asia Printing Solutions Ltd., Dongguan City, Guangdong Province

1 3 5 7 9 10 8 6 4 2

For Fetle Atlaw, who helped us raise a future leader
Love, Gene

How much could these two presidents have in common?

Abraham Lincoln was our sixteenth president. He was a Republican. He was in charge of our country before we had telephones, cars, or lightbulbs. When he was elected, there were only thirty-three states, and our flag had only thirty-three stars.

John Fitzgerald Kennedy was our thirty-fifth president. He was a Democrat. During his presidency one hundred years later, America sent a man into space. Kennedy was the first to be elected under our fifty-star flag.

Both men were named in honor of their grandfathers. Aside from that, they began their lives very differently. Young Abe Lincoln was born on February 12, 1809, near Hodgenville, Kentucky, and raised in a one-room log cabin. There were no modern conveniences.

Abe lived on the frontier and received less than one year of schooling. He had a passion for learning and borrowed books whenever he could.

On May 29, 1917, young John Kennedy was born into the lap of luxury in Brookline, Massachusetts. He had everything a twentieth-century boy could want—except good health. His early years were challenged by whooping cough, measles, and scarlet fever.

John attended elite boarding schools and had private tutors at home when he was ill. Yet he showed little interest in his studies.

Of course, they didn't grow up and immediately become president. They spent a lot of time figuring out who they wanted to be.

There was:

Store Clerk Lincoln,

College Kennedy,

Postmaster Lincoln,

Author and Pulitzer Prize Winner Kennedy,

Attorney Lincoln,

Journalist Kennedy,

and Captain Lincoln of the Illinois militia in the Black Hawk War of 1832.

During World War II, Kennedy was also a military leader. When an enemy ship sank his patrol boat, *PT-109*, Lieutenant Kennedy saved the life of an injured sailor and led his crew on a three-mile swim to safety.

Both men were elected to the U.S. House of Representatives—Lincoln in **1846** and Kennedy in **1946**.

In **1856**, Lincoln was nominated to be a vice presidential candidate, but he lost. In **1956**, Kennedy was also nominated to be a vice presidential candidate. He lost, too. It was a big disappointment for both of them.

LINCOLN

There was plenty to celebrate in their personal lives.

At a local dance in Springfield, Illinois, Lincoln was introduced to a well-educated, charismatic woman named Mary Todd. He said to her, "Miss Todd, I want to dance with you in the worst way." And that's exactly what he did.

KENNEDY

At a small dinner party in Washington, D.C., Kennedy met Jacqueline Bouvier, a smart, ambitious newspaper photographer and journalist. She was engaged to someone else at the time—but not for long.

Lincoln loved nothing more than to tell a good story and make people laugh. Mary looked beyond Lincoln's awkward appearance and recognized his great ambition and intellect.

She fell in love with Kennedy's humor, intelligence, and his competitive nature, which was a true Kennedy trait.

The men did their best to keep personal struggles and tragedies private.

The Lincoln family lost one of their children before the presidency and a second child while in the White House.

Lincoln had already lost his sister, brother, and mother. Throughout his adulthood, he often suffered from depression.

The Kennedy family also lost one of their children before the presidency and a second child while in the White House. Kennedy lost his brother and sister in separate plane accidents.

He lived with a disorder called Addison's disease, which caused weakness and abdominal distress. He also suffered chronic back pain.

Despite the setbacks, Lincoln's and Kennedy's desire and determination to serve our country remained strong.

Lincoln detested slavery. He ran for president against three men, including Stephen A. Douglas and John C. Breckinridge, who wanted slavery to be an option in new states as the country grew.

Northern states agreed with Lincoln; Southern states did not. His critics called him a simple-minded gorilla and made fun of his lanky appearance.

One hundred years later, Jim Crow laws still segregated people based on their race. Descendants of slaves were living without the same rights as white Americans. Kennedy would eventually share Lincoln's vision—equality for all.

He ran for president against Richard M. Nixon. Their debates were the first to be televised. Kennedy won that year, but eight years later, Nixon would win and become president.

Lincoln was elected president of the United States in **1860**. His election was a first of its kind because he was the first president from the newly formed Republican Party. The party's primary goal was to prevent the growth of slavery.

Kennedy was elected president in **1960**. His election was also a first of its kind. He was the first Catholic president. Many feared that a Catholic president would rely on advice from the pope, the leader of the Catholic Church, for government decisions. That was not the case.

There was not a lot of time for Lincoln to celebrate his election. Because the Southern states supported slavery, they decided to split from the North. The United States soon fell apart. Preserving the country became Lincoln's most important concern.

Slave states that originally split

Slave states that split later

Slave states that did not split

Free states

Territories that later became states

Jefferson Davis holding the first Confederate national flag

Robert E. Lee holding the Battle Flag of the Confederacy

The South formed the Confederate States of America and selected Jefferson Davis as its president. Lincoln wanted to reunite the states peacefully. But the Confederates fired the first shot at his Union army and started the Civil War. Robert E. Lee became the South's greatest general and the North's biggest rival.

KENNEDY

When Kennedy entered the White House, he believed our country was threatened by the spread of Communism around the world. Communist governments do not allow the same freedom and opportunities as a democracy, which is the form of government we practice in the United States of America.

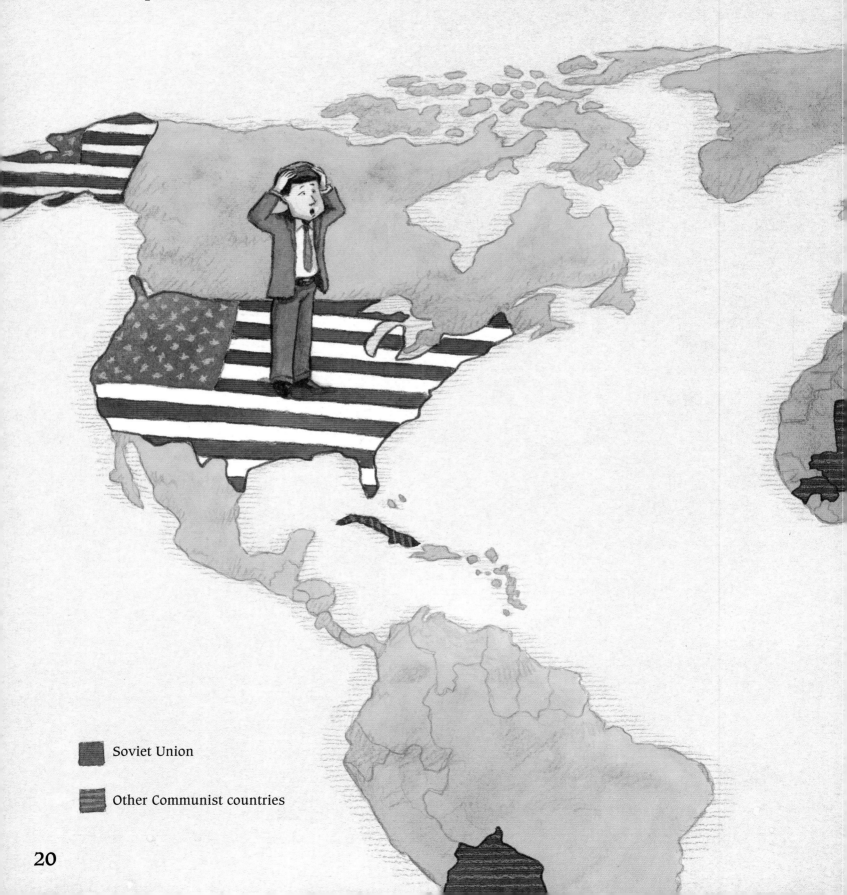

Soviet Union

Other Communist countries

Nikita Khrushchev, the Communist leader of the Soviet Union, was Kennedy's biggest nemesis. Kennedy felt the need to increase his arsenal of nuclear weapons. So did Khrushchev. This power struggle was called the Cold War.

LINCOLN

Both presidencies got off to a rough start. For the first two years of the Civil War, Lincoln's Union army was losing. The war lasted much longer than he ever expected.

Abraham Lincoln

KENNEDY

When Communism moved into Cuba, it was too close for comfort. Kennedy approved an invasion of Cuba to overthrow its leader, Fidel Castro.

John F. Kennedy

Lincoln agonized over the casualties on both sides of the battlefield. In his eyes, every soldier was still an American.

Jefferson Davis

The mission was a complete failure. Castro captured 1,200 men at the Bay of Pigs and remained in power.

Fidel Castro

LINCOLN

Lincoln's goal was to reunite the country. But he changed the focus of the war on January 1, 1863, with the Emancipation Proclamation. It declared freedom for all slaves in Confederate states. Now freed black men could join the Union army and fight to end slavery.

Almost 200,000 black men enlisted by the end of the war.

In 1863, Lincoln met with Frederick Douglass, a former slave who became a leader in the movement to end slavery. For two years, Douglass had publicly criticized Lincoln for not freeing the slaves sooner. He now felt that the president was truly committed to the cause.

In 1963, as black citizens demanded equal rights, they often faced violent protest. Kennedy met with several civil rights leaders, including Martin Luther King Jr., who urged the president to eliminate Jim Crow laws where they still existed.

The Washington Post

Dogs, Fire Hoses Used at Civil Rights March

Kennedy went on TV and the radio to propose new civil rights laws that would end discrimination and injustice for all non-white Americans. King praised the proposal as "the most sweeping and forthright ever presented by an American president."

On June 11, 1963, Kennedy addressed the nation.

"*One hundred years of delay have passed since President Lincoln freed the slaves, yet their heirs . . . are not fully free. They are not yet freed from the bonds of injustice. . . . This Nation . . . will not be fully free until all its citizens are free. . . . Now the time has come for this Nation to fulfill its promise.*"

Lincoln found new hope after his Union army won at the Battle of Gettysburg. His famous Gettysburg Address reminded people why they were fighting.

"Four score and seven years ago our fathers brought forth on this continent, a new nation, conceived in liberty, and dedicated to the proposition that all men are created equal. . . . These dead shall not have died in vain—that this nation, under God, shall have a new birth of freedom—and that government of the people, by the people, for the people, shall not perish from the earth."

In 1962, everything Lincoln fought for almost disappeared during the Cuban Missile Crisis. Khrushchev installed nuclear missiles in Cuba, provoking a confrontation that almost caused a nuclear war. Fortunately, after thirteen tense days, Kennedy could report to America that the two leaders had reached a peaceful resolution.

After four difficult years, Lincoln was elected to a second term. The Union won the Civil War in April 1865. North and South were reunited. He accomplished what he had set out to do. He also persuaded Congress to pass the Thirteenth Amendment to the U.S. Constitution, ending slavery throughout the entire country.

Kennedy continued what Lincoln started when he presented a long-awaited civil rights bill to Congress that later became the Civil Rights Act of 1964. The revolutionary act outlawed segregation and discrimination against people based on their race, religion, or gender.

Then, after such monumental achievements, these two presidents, who enriched the lives of so many, had their lives tragically cut short in two oddly similar assassinations.

- Both were shot on a Friday: Lincoln at Ford's Theatre in Washington, D.C., on April 14, 1865, and Kennedy at Dealey Plaza in Dallas, Texas, on November 22, 1963.
- Both men were sitting beside their wives, who were not hurt.
- A second man was injured in the attack on each president.

- Lincoln was shot in Ford's Theatre; Kennedy was shot riding in a Lincoln (made by the Ford Motor Company).
- Both assassins used three names: John Wilkes Booth shot Lincoln, and Lee Harvey Oswald shot Kennedy.
- Both assassins were killed before their trials.
- Both presidents were succeeded by men named Johnson. Andrew Johnson was born in 1808; Lyndon B. Johnson was born in 1908.
- Kennedy's funeral ceremonies were modeled after Lincoln's services.

Kennedy has a final resting place in Arlington National Cemetery in Virginia. It overlooks the Lincoln Memorial.

The legacies of President Abraham Lincoln and President John F. Kennedy continue to inspire new generations.

WHAT WILL YOUR LEGACY BE?

WHILE IN OFFICE

★ He declared Thanksgiving a national holiday.

★ He signed into law the Homestead Act, which encouraged people to move to western territories by offering them land if they lived on it for five years or more.

    ★ He approved the Freedmen's Bureau, which assisted freed slaves with food, medical care, and legal services.

    ★ He authorized the first transcontinental railroad to connect the East and West Coasts.

    ★ He started the U.S. Department of Agriculture to promote farming; it now serves consumers with food-assistance and food-inspection programs.

TRIVIA

★ Lincoln was the first president to be born outside the original thirteen states.

★ He hated the name "Abe" and preferred to be called "Mr. President" or just "Lincoln."

★ Lincoln first offered Robert E. Lee command of the Union forces.

★ After the 1860 election, serious death threats led Lincoln to wear a disguise and sneak into Washington, D.C., for his inauguration.

★ About a year before John Wilkes Booth shot Abraham Lincoln, Booth's brother Edwin saved the life of a man he did not know. It was Lincoln's son Robert.

QUOTES

★ *A house divided against itself cannot stand. I believe this government cannot endure, permanently half slave and half free.*

★ *Upon the subject of education . . . I can only say that I view it as the most important subject which we as a people can be engaged in.*

★ *I have never had a feeling politically that did not spring from the sentiments embodied in the Declaration of Independence.*

★ *The man does not live who is more devoted to peace than I am. None who would do more to preserve it.*

★ *Let us have faith that right makes might, and in that faith, let us, to the end, dare to do our duty as we understand it.*

WHILE IN OFFICE

★ He started the Peace Corps, which sends people to work overseas as volunteers in developing communities.

★ He initiated the space program to land a man on the moon.

★ He signed the Equal Pay Act to ensure women fair pay in the workplace.

★ He pushed for the first Clean Air Act to help control and prevent air pollution.

★ Kennedy wanted to prevent Communism from taking over South Vietnam, so he sent troops and advisers. It began our involvement in the Vietnam War.

TRIVIA

★ His friends and family called him Jack. His wife, Jacqueline, was called Jackie.

★ With his home-movie camera, an onlooker named Zapruder happened to film Kennedy's assassination. "The Zapruder Film" is the most complete recording of the historic event. The onlooker's first name? Abraham.

★ At the age of forty-three, he was the youngest president ever elected to office. He followed President Dwight D. Eisenhower, who at the time was the oldest president ever, at age seventy.

★ After the Cuban Missile Crisis, the first hotline between the United States and the Soviet Union was installed to avoid future communication problems.

★ During his time in the White House, he gave all of his presidential salary to charity.

QUOTES

★ *My fellow Americans, ask not what your country can do for you—ask what you can do for your country.*

★ *Let us not seek the Republican answer or the Democratic answer but the right answer. Let us not seek to fix the blame for the past—let us accept our own responsibility for the future.*

★ *Too often we . . . enjoy the comfort of opinion without the discomfort of thought.*

★ *The great enemy of the truth is very often not the lie . . . but the myth, persistent, persuasive, and unrealistic.*

★ *If we cannot end now our differences, at least we can help make the world safe for diversity.*

GLOSSARY

Bay of Pigs—A bay on the south coast of Cuba where U.S.-trained Cuban exiles landed in 1961 to overthrow Fidel Castro's Communist government. The invasion was a failure.

Civil Rights Act of 1964—A law proposed by John F. Kennedy and later signed by President Lyndon B. Johnson that outlawed discrimination against people based on their race, color, religion, or gender.

Civil War—The war fought from 1861 to 1865 between America's Northern states and eleven Southern states that seceded and formed the Confederate States of America. Lincoln fought to reunite North and South.

Cold War—A political power struggle between the United States and the Soviet Union that started after World War II and lasted much of the century. The confrontations almost led to a nuclear war during Kennedy's presidency.

Communism—A system of government that strictly controls the lives of its citizens and owns all means of producing goods and services, including land and factories. The people are not represented in the government.

Democracy—A system of government in which people elect leaders to make decisions on their behalf.

Emancipation Proclamation—An executive order made by President Abraham Lincoln to free slaves in Confederate-controlled states.

House of Representatives—One of the two houses of the U.S. Congress that create laws. The number of representatives each state has is determined by its population size.

Jim Crow laws—From 1877 to 1965, these laws did not give black people the same civil rights as white people, allowing racial segregation in the South.

Segregate—To keep people apart based on their race, color, religion, or gender.

Thirteenth Amendment—An addition to the U.S. Constitution that abolished slavery in the United States.

U.S. Constitution—The founding document of the United States that establishes the fundamental framework of the government and outlines many rights of the people.

SOURCES

Abraham and Mary Lincoln: A House Divided. American Experience/PBS, 2005. 360 min.

Adler, Bill, ed. *The Uncommon Wisdom of JFK: A Portrait in His Own Words*. New York: Rugged Land, 2003.

Fleming, Thomas. *JFK's War*. Boston: New Word City, 2014.

Freedman, Russell. *Abraham Lincoln and Frederick Douglass: The Story Behind an American Friendship*. New York: Clarion, 2012.

Goodwin, Doris Kearns. *Team of Rivals: The Political Genius of Abraham Lincoln*. New York: Simon & Schuster, 2006.

Keneally, Thomas. *Abraham Lincoln*. New York: Viking, 2003.

The Kennedys. American Experience/PBS, 2003. 240 min.

Kenney, Charles. *John F. Kennedy: The Presidential Portfolio; History As Told Through the Collection of the John F. Kennedy Library and Museum*. New York: PublicAffairs, 2000.

Lincoln. The History Channel/A&E Home Video, 2006. 140 min.

The Presidents: The Lives and Legacies of the 43 Leaders of the United States. The History Channel/A&E Home Video, 2005. 360 min.